Living the Best Me Beyond the Crazy You

Kim,
"Live the Best you"
Blessing
Cis

Living the Best Me Beyond the Crazy You

Iris Cockrell

ISBN: 978-0-615-24705-2

All Scripture quotations, unless otherwise indicated, are taken from the
Holy Bible, New International Version®, NIV®, Copyright© 1973, 1978,
1984 by International Bible Society. Used by permission of Zondervan. All
rights reserved.
Psalm 139:13-16 New King James Translation
Psalm 139:13-16 New Living Translation
Psalm 139:13-16 New Life Version
Ephesians 3:20 Amplified Bible

Cover design, interior design, and printing by Bethany Press International
(www.bethanypress.com)

Printed in the United States of America.

DEDICATION

To the women of the past who struggled
everyday to survive and did so,
Against all odds

To the women of the present who are struggling
everyday to survive and will do so,
Against all odds

$\mathcal{A}$CKNOWLEDGMENTS

$\mathcal{L}$ ord Jesus, I love you and I thank you for giving me life. I am so grateful for all the opportunities you give me to share the gospel with others. I bless you for giving me the vision and the ability to write this book to your honor and glory.

To my husband, Wayne, thank you for giving me the privilege to resign from the job and pursue the vision God placed in my heart to write this book. Thank you for your love, prayers, encouragement, support and money (smile). Thank you for being there for me and believing in me. I love you.

My children, Wayne Jr., Maria (who is my cheerleader), Marcus, and my daughter-in-law, Zena, thank you for your love, encouragement and prayers. I love you. Christian, Dante' and Sidnee, my grandchildren, thank you for all the big hugs and kisses you give Moni. I love you more.

To two very special women in my life, my mother, Anna Harper, who loves me and supports me with all her heart, and my mother-in-law, Mary Reins, who loved me the first day she met me. Both of you have imparted wisdom, encouragement and given me strength to accomplish everything I ever attempted to do in life. Thank you for being testimonies for God.

A special thank you to my sisters, Debbie, Ingrid, Felicia, my brother, Mann, and my sister-in-laws, Sandy and Monica, for always being there for me.

To my dear circle of true friends, thank you for believing in me, praying for me and speaking positive affirmations into my heart.

Contents

INTRODUCTION

How do I live the best me beyond the crazy you? The demands of life are pushing women into the red zone. I call the red zone a space of heightened anxiety. When women are living in this space they often learn to operate the events of the day in their own strength. The danger of living in the red zone can cause headaches, body pains, sleeplessness, frustration, anger, jitters, hair loss, wrinkles, tiredness, stomach aches, hives, blemishes and a host of ailments too numerous to name. In this fast-paced chaotic society we are living in today dealing with crazy people, crazy circumstances, and the crazy melodrama we find ourselves encountering everyday, you may wonder if it's possible to live the best me beyond all this.

Women have so many demands placed upon them today that it is becoming almost impossible to maintain the essentials for living the best you. Women are wearing and changing so many hats throughout the day. They are taking care of the jobs, taking care of the husbands, taking care of the children, taking care of the grandchildren, taking care of parents, taking care of church ministries, taking care of bills, taking care of the groceries, taking care of the family doctor visits, taking care of the dog or cat, taking care of the car, taking children to practices, cleaning the house, and meeting the demands of a job outside or inside the home. They are taking care of everyone and everything except themselves. Not to mention having their own personal struggles with self-esteem, strongholds of the mind, health issues, weight management, and making time for God. When night falls all they can do is go to bed without a thought as to, "How did I take care of me today"? And then wake up the next morning to the same hectic routine.

Sisters, we have lost the art of taking care of ourselves. It is very important to remember you within your hectic lifestyle. We have overextended ourselves and are afraid to admit it and too afraid to ask for help, because if we do, it gives the impression that we are not smart enough or strong enough to carry our load. As a result, we are falling apart at the seams and when we realize this it is because some event has happened in our lives to get our attention, shake us up, or wake us up before it is too late. Now is the time to begin looking at ways to live the best you, despite all the craziness. There are always going to be crazy people in your life. People will always try to impose physiological issues upon your mind. There will always be crazy circumstances because stuff happens, and crazy melodrama because you have your own personal issues.

Circumstances that are out of your control you must leave in the caring hands of God. But the things you can take control of and change, you must take them by force through prayer, faith, and action. It is imperative for you to begin to put your faith into action if you are going to experience living the best you. The things you will read in this book will serve as an encouragement and reminder to you of the wonderful God we serve and His desire for you to be successful in everything He created you to be.

As I was approaching my fiftieth birthday I took inventory of my life. I examined every aspect of it to see if I, indeed, was living the best me. Was I truly living the life God intended for me to live? I made it personal, not about anyone else's life, but my life. This caused me to dig deep within myself and be honest with me. I found areas that needed to be overhauled, improved, discovered, rediscovered, cleaned up, cleaned out and reinvented. And this could only happen by submitting to God's Word and making changes according to His Word. My heart's desire is that you will draw from some of my experiences and allow God to provoke change in you so that you will begin living the best you. Begin living out the woman He created you to live, apart from anyone's opinion or desires for your life. Remember you are the only you.

1

*C*HANGE THE DIAL ON THE CHANNEL

an you name that tune? Woe is me, Woe is me, and Woe is me. Have you been listening to the same old station for so long that you have forgotten how to change the dial? Everyday you say the same old things to yourself. You are singing the same old song you have sung for the majority of your life. You think the same old way about life that you have either been taught to think or learned to think based on the circumstances life has presented to you. Do theses notes sound familiar to you? When I was a child I was abandoned, I developed poor self-esteem, nobody really loves me, you know we were poor growing up, you know I am not married because my ex-husband was no good, people always hurt me, I don't trust anyone. Woe is me, Woe is me, and Woe is me. I am sure if you cannot identify with any of these, you have your own unique tune you sing for the whole world to hear.

Every time you start a conversation you have to remind the person you are talking to what has happened to you in the past. This is a good testimony if you ever get to the deliverance and victory part of the testimony. But for some reason you never get past the misfortune or hurts and pains. I hear this all the time. You are stuck in a negative pattern of thinking and it is holding you prisoner. The negative thoughts have imbedded themselves so deeply upon the canvas of your mind you have become a prisoner to your own mind. Just the very mention of possibly changing your thought patterns unnerves you. The memories of the past are preventing you from moving forward. You wake up thinking of the past. You go to bed thinking of the past. Perhaps this is your moment. Perhaps you have desired to break this cycle and just didn't know where to start.

If you are going to begin living the best you, you must change the dial on the channel and begin to sing a new song. Change is made by a choice. Granted you have experienced some terrible things in your life and so have I. Everyday you have the ability and the power to change your thoughts by choosing what you will meditate on. What thoughts you will allow to control your mind.

I have always wanted a Bose radio because the sound is clear and crisp. You can hear every note of the instruments playing. When I got the radio I programmed all of my favorite stations on it. All I have to do is press the button on the remote control to choose a station to listen to. One day I discovered that I had programmed the same station on two different channels. I thought, "Why did I do that"? Then I remembered the listening stations that I liked were limited so I programmed them twice. How many stations have I programmed in my mind that continue to play everyday at the thought of a memory, or when I am disappointed, or when I am discouraged, or when things just are not going my way or the way I think they should go? I wondered. I discovered I had been playing the same stations for a very long time.

The tunes on my listening stations were tunes of regret, hurt, discouragement, rejection, fear and loneliness. They had developed a harmonious symphony that crescendos at the thought of disillusionments. I discovered that although the circumstances in my life had changed, my thought patterns had not. I had become stuck in a rut of thinking that was not consistent with the Word of God. I asked myself, am I living the best me God intended for me? I realized it was not so important to dwell on how I got stuck but how I was going to come out of the rut. How was I going to reprogram the listening stations of my mind?

I had an intuitive grasp of reality as I was watching a wedding show on television. As the daughter came out of the dressing room in her beautiful wedding gown, her parents became so overwhelmed with emotion at the realization that they were giving their daughter away in marriage, they began to cry as they were smiling. I thought, what are you crying for? She is beginning a new life with someone she loves, please! But what God revealed to me was that this was a good memory in their life. Here was my breakthrough. I needed to change the channel on the programmed stations I had been listening to and begin reflecting on the good memories God had allowed me to experience in my life—memories that bring a smile to my face and heart. The bad memories made me sad, drained my energy, and caused me to lose my focus in the moments of life. Oh, how I was missing blessing in this state of being. I prayed and asked God to help me remember all the good memories I had experienced in my life and let them replace the bad memories.

Holding on to bad memories tends to be easy. It is hard to forget the pain someone caused you when that pain has pierced deep into the center of your heart in a place you did not know existed. Talk about having physiological issues. Wow! Granted, I have not totally forgotten all of the bad memories I have experienced and most likely I will not, but knowing I have the power through the Holy Spirit who dwells inside of me, I can quickly check the bad memories when they want to dominate my thoughts and replace them with the good memories I have experienced in my life.

Then I wondered if the problem could be that we experience more bad memories in life than good memories. A bad experience can trap your mind in prison for the rest of your life if you let it. Perhaps what God intended as learning lessons in our life we have interpreted as bad if they caused us pain. It took me some time to grasp the concept that God would allow things to hurt me so that He could grow me. But it has been in my deepest hurts and pain that I drew closer to God and He drew closer to me. It has been through some of my painful experiences that God has revealed gifts and talents to me. God is still God and we forget He was there in the bad moments as well as the good moments. So I decided if I was going to become victorious over my thoughts, I had to retrain my brain to think on the good memories God had allowed me to experience every time I thought of the bad memories, however they were provoked.

2 Corinthians 10:5-6 says: *We demolish arguments and every pretension that sets itself up against the knowledge of God, and we take captive every thought to make it obedient to Christ. And we will be ready to punish every act of disobedience, once your obedience is complete.*

When you take captive of the bad memory, you take the power and control away from the stronghold because you choose not to dwell on that memory anymore. You then give yourself permission to replace it with the good memories and the good ones to come. I found that every good memory made me smile. You try it. Think of a good memory and watch, you'll smile. Um-hm, I told you. When you smile you make your heart smile and you pass that along to others. The more you meditate on the good memories of your life the more you will begin to cultivate fertile soil for positive reactions to other people. When you dwell all day on bad memories and encounter other people, you pass all that negative energy on to them. In other words, you will not walk around with your gun loaded ready to shoot every person who passes your way, but what will project from your spirit will be a reflection of what you have been thinking about. This is a daily, thought by thought rehearsal, and you have to continue to do it. Let me warn you there are days when applying this practice will be a true struggle and when I am having one of those days my defense is the Word of God. I meditate upon Philippians 4:8, *Finally, brothers, whatever is true, whatever is noble, whatever is right, whatever is pure, whatever is lovely,* whatever *is admirable—if anything is excellent or praiseworthy—think about such things.* True JESUS, Noble JESUS, Right JESUS, Pure JESUS, Lovely JESUS, Admirable JESUS, Excellent JESUS, Praiseworthy JESUS, Think about Jesus. Change the dial on the channel and get a new station, sister. You have been singing that tune for too long. I have a new dial on my station that's called FREE THOUGHTS, and the song titles played are these:

That was then; this is now, it's a new day.
But God said.
Yesterday I was full of sorrow, but today I am full of joy.
My memories have become my strength.
It's a new day with a fresh hope.
God's plan is my purpose.
I am more than a conqueror.
I have victory in Jesus
I am a child of the King
I am walking in my authority
I will bless the Lord at all times.

Now you change the dial on your station and write some new songs. Sing, girl, Sing! Do you understand the power of changing your thoughts? It is a choice and you have the ability and the power to change your thoughts. God encourages us through Paul's life in Philippians 3:13. He said, *forgetting those things that are behind to attain those things which are ahead.*

Forgetting is defined as: *retention loss, which refers to the apparent loss of information already encoded and stored in an individual's long-term memory.* It is a spontaneous or gradual process in which old memories are unable to be recalled from memory storage.

Ahead is defined as: *in a forward direction or position, in front or for the future <plan ahead> in or toward a more advantageous position.*

God is telling you that in order to change the dial on the station and sing a new song you must develop retention loss of the old memories and redirect your thinking to a new position. Here lies your deliverance from the bondage of bad memories. It is time to set your mind free. Try it! What is the worst that could happen? You have nothing to lose and everything to gain. Romans 12:2b says, *Be transformed by the renewing of your mind.* Change the dial on the channel and sing a new song. Now it's your turn to sing. Sing, Sister! Sing. Write yourself some new songs.

Self Reflections/Group Discussion

1. What are some of the same tunes you find yourself singing everyday?

    _____

    _____

    _____

    _____

2. List as many good memories that you can remember and reflect on them.

    _____

    _____

    _____

    _____

3. Read Philippians 3:13. What is God saying to you?

    _____

    _____

    _____

    _____

4. What life lessons have you considered a bad memory?

    _____

    _____

    _____

    _____

5. Write your new song.

    _____

    _____

    _____

    _____

2

*S*HHH, I CAN'T HEAR YOU

*J*ust think for a moment, that God almighty, the creator of heaven and earth who called darkness to light, placed the sun and moon in the sky, named the stars, put the birds in the air, placed the fish in the sea, made man in His own image, breathed the breath of life into man, created woman from a rib, and redeemed you from your sins by Christ Jesus, desires to talk to you. God desires to talk to you, the woman He created from the blueprint of His heart, a blueprint so specific there is no one else on the face of the earth like you nor will there ever be another woman like you. God deserves a shout of praise right now for the marvelous design He created, you. When God created you He wanted to have fellowship with you through communication. Almighty God desires to talk to you. But there is a problem.

Your surroundings are so loud with the cares of doing, moving, and going, that you are not hearing God speak to you. Most women are comfortable in their own home, they know who they are, they turn on the television, or the radio, get on the computer, or start talking on the telephone, prepare dinner, attend to the children, or other duties, but they can't hear God speak. They can't really identify God's voice. They know their children's voices, their husband's voice, their boyfriend's voice, their girlfriend's voice, their co-worker's voice; they even know various artists when they sing. They say, oh, girl, that is so and so, and anyone else they frequently talk to, but they are confused and not sure when God is speaking to them because they cannot recognize the tone of His voice. In John 10:4, Jesus said: *When he has brought out all his own, he goes on ahead of them, and his sheep follow him because they know his voice.* In order to hear God's voice you have to be listening for it. What are you listening for? What is dominating your eardrums?

Everyday I have to settle myself down to talk to God and listen for Him to talk to me. My life and the people in my life can get rather crazy. I have to get alone, be still and listen for God to speak to my heart. There are days when He doesn't say a word to me but I create an atmosphere to be in His presence to listen. If you desire to hear God speak to you it is necessary for you to become quiet. Being absolutely quiet frightens some women. I believe the fear of absolute silence is due to several reasons. Perhaps you grew up in a loud home, or maybe quiet to you denotes loneliness, or you feel a sense of isolation when it is quiet.

Once your environment has been quieted, and your heart and mind are still, you will be able to re-center, refocus and reconnect with God. When you re-center yourself you come into the Lord's presence in humility. Your focus is now on Him and you are able to reconnect in the Spirit with the Lord. This can be done no other way. Jesus said, *My sheep hear my voice.* Have you ever been in a crowd and heard someone call your name? The first thing you do is stop and say, "Someone just called my name". If you are with someone, you ask them if they heard someone call your name. You hear them call you again. This time you stop and look around and see that someone is waving trying to get your attention. But you heard someone call you. Jesus is calling to you right now but you can't hear Him.

It is imperative for you to know God's voice if you are going to become successful in your relationship with Him, otherwise you will have a one-way relationship with the Lord based on your requests alone. Therefore you will miss opportunities to do His will.

I have learned the voice of God and it is no secret to me and it should be no mysterious secret to you in learning how God's voice sounds to you. You must understand it is personal. It is a personal communication from God to you. God speaks to me in a quiet whisper. It took me a moment or two to identify His tone. I remember praying and asking God to speak to me. I would say:

"Dear Lord, I want to hear your voice, I want to identify your tone. I desire to hear what you are saying to me, not others. Teach me to recognize your voice."

Everyone has a character tone in their voice. There is a pitch that is recognizable when you frequently talk to someone. I thought, perhaps, I would hear this deep, bold, body-shaking scream in my ear but, instead, I began to hear whispers deep on the inside of my soul. I am very good at talking to God. I can give God a list that could keep Him busy for at least a year with one request. I began to realize that there are times everyone has an opinion or suggestion concerning your life. You will always find yourself in the decision process concerning issues of life. Sometimes people can't help you. But, above all, I began to desire to hear from God. I would hear a whisper say, do this and I would say, what? Hmm, where did that come from? There were times I ignored that whisper, but when I did, later that day, next week, or next month I would have a revelation that would drop me to my knees. "Oh, no", God, you spoke to me about that. You told me what to do and I rejected what you said because I was not sure of the whisper. That's when I realized God *was* speaking to me. He was speaking to the depth of my soul in a whisper and now I know his voice. So, when I hear the quiet whisper, I react and do what He says even when it doesn't make sense to me, and it never does, even when it causes me pain, and most of the time it does, even when it makes me look stupid in the eyes of others, and I am sure it does, even when I don't want to, most often I don't. But it works, every time I obey His voice it strengthens my heart in trusting Him. Now faith is the substance of things hoped for and the evidence of things not seen. When I obey God's voice my faith is strengthened in the things I am hoping for, though I can't visualize them happening right now I know He is able to bring my hopes to pass.

God's voice is the sweetest voice I have ever heard. His voice is not harsh but stern, not bitter but gentle, not dogmatic but authoritative, not derogative but encouraging, always guiding with a love that brings about life-changing results. Every time He speaks directly to me it changes my life. You will never have an experience in this life greater than hearing God speak to you.

I love it when God talks to me. Perhaps He will not whisper to you, but how will you ever know if you don't start making time to hear His voice? How will you learn the distinct tone in His voice for you? Now is the time for you to quiet yourself down and create an atmosphere conducive to recognizing God's voice. Because when you recognize His voice your life will never be the same, you will be clear on carrying out the assignment He has given you to do without confusion. When you are able to identify God's voice the devil cannot talk you out of your assignment. When you hear God's voice, other people will not be able to persuade you to change the assignment God has given you, but there will be a continued calming in your soul about what you are doing and where you are going as you listen to Him. You will develop a confidence about life that will provoke change because you can now hear God speak to you.

God speaks to me through His Word also. Psalm 119:130 says, *The unfolding of your words gives light; it gives understanding to the simple.* You don't have to be afraid or smart to read and study the Word of God. Did you read the promise God gave us concerning His Word? You have to first enter into the Bible; that means pick it up and open it up. Are you quick to lay your Bible down after Sunday worship services and then not pick it up again until church? God has promised to give you understanding of the word you are reading, so don't be intimidated when reading and studying the Bible. God said, "I will give you understanding". It takes time and discipline to read and study the Word of God. I have to make time and discipline myself for this. I identified where I had been wasting time and then began to devote that time to reading and studying the Bible. Now is the time for you to begin to identify wasted time in your daily activities and devote it to reading and studying the Bible. You have to discipline yourself to make time. No one can do this for you.

God has spoken to me through His Word on many issues time and time again. There have been times when I just did not know what to do, how, or if I should do it. In times of distress, confusion, and heartbreak, the Bible has been my salvation in life issues. After all the counseling sessions, after all the advice from friends, and after all the book readings for answers to your life, no matter what, you will only find answers to your life in the Bible. Psalm 143:8 says: *Let the morning bring me word of your unfailing love, for I have put my trust in you. Show me the way I should go, for to you I lift up my soul.*

God desires that you know Him also through His Word. There are so many truths and promises in the Word of God that it is imperative to read and study the Bible. When you do, you understand more and more of God's heart. It is exciting when I am reading the Word of God and the words jump off the page. The Word of God makes an impact upon my heart that is like nothing I can describe. Sisters, it is time to move from the one-paragraph devotionals to the Bible. Don't get me wrong, devotionals are okay and they have their place in our lives, but they should not override reading and studying the Bible. A devotional is a scripture from the Bible and then thought is given to the scripture by one's opinion or experience. The Bible is God's instructional to mankind. God took pen and wrote from the depths of His heart to us.

2 Peter 1:2-3 says: *Grace and peace be yours in abundance through the knowledge of God and of Jesus our Lord. His divine power has given us everything we need for life and godliness through our knowledge of Him who called us by His own glory and goodness.* When you read and study the Word of God you began to understand how to apply the knowledge of the truth to your situations. God has given you everything you need to do this through His Word. When you begin to apply the knowledge of truth you will be able to minimize your time living in the red zone. Here is where the rubber meets the road in application. There is no grey area, either you are going to do what God says or you're not.

Life will hit you with some situations that will make you want to run away, hurt somebody, say things, or do things that you know are wrong. It is the knowledge of the Word of God, and the examples that our Lord Jesus Christ has left for you to follow, when applied (meaning when you choose to obey what God says) will sustain you and keep you focused when you're trapped in the Red Sea, water surrounding you, and it appears you will be overtaken by the rushing of mighty waters. The Word of God never changes. In Malachi 3:6, God said: *For I am the Lord, I do not change; Therefore you are not consumed.* (NKJV) God never changes. Praise Him. People will change, circumstances will change, you will change, but God remains consistent because He is the ONLY. He said I Am who I Am. No matter what changes in life, He never changes. What He has declared in the Word will remain truth and true to the end of time.

God is faithful to His Word and He cannot lie. He is the only stabilizing force in your life. That is why you have not been consumed. The word *consumed* means: *to do away with completely: DESTROY.* There will never be a situation in your life designed by God to destroy you. No matter how bad it seems, how hopeless it looks, God is on your side. God gives this wonderful promise. Jeremiah 29:11 says, *"For I know the plans I have for you"*, declares the Lord, *"plans to prosper you and not to harm you, plans to give you hope and a future."*

God has spoken in His Word and desires that you read His words. God has so many things He wants to say to you. Spending time listening for God to speak to you and reading the Word of God will revive you, it will retrieve you from destruction, it will relieve you of your cares, and it will remind you who God is. Sister, each day God gives you to experience life is a gift from Him. Stop wasting time on things that won't amount to anything after it is all over. Start today, right now. Reconnect with the Lord your God. Shhhhhhhh, quiet down, be still, re-center, reconnect, and refocus. He is waiting ever so patiently to talk to you.

Self Reflections/Group Discussion

1. Identify your atmosphere. Do you have a quiet place to meet with God?

   _____

   _____

   _____

   _____

2. How do you prepare yourself to hear from God?

   _____

   _____

   _____

   _____

3. Can you recognize God's voice?

   _____

   _____

   _____

   _____

4. Did I read my Bible today, or yesterday? Don't remember? Why?

   _____

   _____

   _____

   _____

5. List ways you will reconnect with God.

   _____

   _____

   _____

   _____

3

SET YOURSELF FREE, FORGIVENESS

There is absolutely no way you are going to journey through this life without practicing forgiveness. People will hurt you and you will hurt people; therefore, the need for forgiveness is necessary. In Luke 11:2-4 Jesus said this is how you ought to pray. He said to them, "When you pray, say:

'Father, hallowed be your name,
your kingdom come.
Give us each day our daily bread.
Forgive us our sins,
for we also forgive everyone who sins against us.
And lead us not into temptation.' "

There are going to be times that you will be hurt and mistreated by others. Sometimes the pain will be so deep you will question if you can ever forgive. We need God's forgiveness every minute of the day. We sin against Him and He desires to forgive us when we ask Him, but we are not so quick to forgive others.

When I gave my life to Jesus and accepted His atonement for my sins, I thought everything was going to be golden in my life, only to find out later my greatest test of forgiveness was going to come from those in the body of Christ. In my natural family I knew how to settle things. My siblings and I fought all the time but by nightfall we were back to being sisters and brothers laughing and joking again. The friends I had before I was saved spoke their mind and I spoke mine. After the disagreement and cuss down we were cool again. But in the family of God it seems to be quite different. You will find that every sin committed against you before you were saved has the same potential after you are saved, and from the people with whom you closely associate.

David experienced this. Read Psalm 41:9, *Even my close friend, whom I trusted, he who shared my bread, has lifted up his heel against me.* Psalm 55:12-14, *If an enemy were insulting me, I could endure it; if a foe were raising himself against me, I could hide from him. But it is you, a man like myself, my companion, my close friend, with whom I once enjoyed sweet fellowship as we walked with the throng at the house of God.* Can you identify with David's pain? I know I can.

When we hurt we hurt. In our hurt we tend to forget this portion of God's Word, forgive us our sins, for we also forgive everyone who sins against us.

God said to forgive others and He will forgive you. The word, *forgive* means *to cease to feel resentment against.* Okay, I know you just got a rush. Someone entered your mind just from that definition. When you thought about that person it made you sick. The sight of them makes you want to hurt them. Just to think they could do such a thing to you and appear to be getting away with it. Now, God said, "This one I want you to forgive. I want you to forgive them as I have forgiven you." You must choose to obey what God says: forgive them as I have forgiven you. Matthew 18:15 says, *"If your brother sins against you, go and show him his fault, just between the two of you. If he listens to you, you have won your brother over".* What do you do when someone does not agree that they have sinned against you? Forgive them. What do you do when you never got an opportunity to tell them they hurt you? Forgive them.

Even after you have forgiven someone sometimes the space inside your heart that has harbored the pain for so long is still active. I call it residue. An example of residue is your charcoal grill.

When you fire up the charcoals and get them red hot you cook the food. After the coals cool you clean out the bottom of the charcoal grill. After getting all the charcoal out there is still a little residue of ash left on the bottom that is too cumbersome to get out, so you leave it. But after some time, if you don't get it out, it will harden onto the bottom of the grill and you will need a chisel to get it up.

This is what settles in our hearts after we say I forgive you. You say I have forgiven you but from time to time you find yourself thinking of what they did, how they did it, and why they did it to you. This rehearsal is the residue that is lying deep on the bottom of your heart. Things that happened to you when you were a child that still make you cry today, it is residue. Your husband is dead but you still cry over the things he did or did not do to you, it is residue. You are working on a new job but you still carry the hurts from the previous job, it is residue. Family members have turned their back on you and you still crying, it is residue. You have remarried and your new husband does something that reminds you of your former husband and you fly off the handle, it is residue.

So how do you get rid of the residue? We all carry residue. It seems the deeper the hurt the more residue. If you do not deal with the residue it will have a stronghold in your heart and mind that can potentially control your thoughts and actions toward the person you have forgiven. When the residue rises to the surface you can't ignore it, you have to deal with it. Ephesians 4: 29-32 says: *Do not let any unwholesome talk come out of your mouths, but only what is helpful for building others up according to their needs, that it may benefit those who listen. And do not grieve the Holy Spirit of God, with whom you were sealed for the day of redemption. Get rid of all bitterness, rage and anger, brawling and slander, along with every form of malice. Be kind and compassionate to one another, forgiving each other, just as in Christ God forgave you.*

The Holy Spirit brings the residue to the surface for you to deal with because it grieves Him. In order for you to be kind and compassionate you must get rid of the bitterness, rage, and anger by submitting yourself to God. When the residue is bought to the surface you need help to get rid of it. 1 Peter 5:6-7 says, *Humble yourselves, therefore, under God's mighty hand, that he may lift you up in due time. Cast all your anxiety on him because he cares for you.* Humble yourself and tell God you need His help to get rid of the residue. I love this verse because after you have humbled yourself and asked God for help, He gives you an invitation to cast all your cares upon Him. What a mighty God! God wants to take the residue so He can work out in you the good work He has placed in you.

So, you made it through this hurt and just when you think you have arrived, just when your heart and mind is clear, just when you are applying the principles of God's Word to your life and you say, "Lord, I thank you I got over this one", before you blink your eyes you are clipped from behind and the cycle starts all over again. And you say to yourself, "Oh, no, not this time. I am not dealing with this again". Look at what Jesus says to the disciples in Matthew 18:21-22: *Then, Peter came to Jesus and asked, "Lord, how many times shall I forgive my brother when he sins against me? Up to seven times?" Jesus answered, "I tell you, not seven times, but seventy-seven times."* Luke 17:4-5 says, *"If he sins against you seven times in a day, and seven times comes back to you and says, 'I repent', forgive him." The apostles said to the Lord, "Increase our faith!"*

Perhaps you are struggling with forgiving yourself. Not only do you have to forgive others but you have to forgive yourself. For whatever issue you are holding yourself prisoner, now is the time to let it go. As long as you hold onto it you will never experience all the blessing God has in store for you. When you have forgiven yourself then you have freed yourself. When you give yourself permission to release the guilt and pain of past things you have done that were not profitable, then you are in a position to set yourself free through the blood of Jesus. You are hurting right now because you refuse to forgive yourself. Galatians 5:1 says: *It is for freedom that Christ has set us free. Stand firm, then, and do not let yourselves be burdened again by a yoke of slavery.* You can let it go; you are free in Christ Jesus.

God says to you in Isaiah 43:25, *I am He who blots out your transgressions for my own sake, and I will not remember your sins.*

This was a difficult chapter for me to write. When I began this chapter I stopped and said, "God, you don't want this here. Give me something else to write about that will help my sisters." I got up from my computer and did not return for two days. I cried, begged, and pleaded with God to give me something else to write. I was bombarded with satanic attacks and then I knew for sure I was to write this to you. During those two days God broke my hardened heart and I was able to forgive some people that I had held prisoners in my heart. It was a choice of obedience. But I tell you this, when you forgive others and yourself, there is a freedom in your soul. A weight lifts off your shoulders, and a power rises up on the inside of you that allows you to love even that one.

Forgiveness is a mandatory discipline for the woman of God. Forgiveness is a daily struggle of obedience, but I am learning the quicker I practice forgiving others and myself, God is well-pleased. When I obey what God says, then I have the permission and the authority from God to ask, "Give me this day my daily bread". I know it doesn't make sense; it never does but, guess what, it works every time.

Self Reflections/Group Discussion

1. Who do you need to forgive? Why?

   _____

   _____

   _____

   _____

2. Do you have residue?

   _____

   _____

   _____

   _____

3. How is residue affecting you?

   _____

   _____

   _____

   _____

4. Read Ephesians 4: 29-32. What is God saying to you?

   _____

   _____

   _____

   _____

5. Pray a prayer of forgiveness to God. Ask God to forgive you of your sins. Ask God to help you forgive those who have hurt you.

   _____

   _____

   _____

   _____

4

MIRROR, MIRROR ON THE WALL

Mirror, Mirror, on the wall, the back of the door, in my purse, or on either side of my car door, tell me, is it true, am I the fairest of them all? Well, I don't like what I see, and I don't like who I am. I am too fat, I am too skinny, I am ugly, I am too dark, I am too light, I'm not smart enough, I stutter, I am too short, I am too tall, I have freckles, I have zits, my hands are too big, my hands are too little, I have large breasts, I have little breasts, I have big feet, I have a large nose, my ears are big, my teeth are bucked, I have big lips, I have skinny lips, my eyes are too big, my eyes are too small, my eyebrows are too thin, my eyebrows are too thick, my forehead is big, my butt is too big, I don't have a butt, my hair is thin, I am bald, I don't have a husband, I don't have a car, I don't have a house, I don't have children, I don't have a boyfriend, I don't have a college degree, I don't have a high school diploma, I have a crappy job, I am not loved, I am not liked, and I just struggle with who I am. So, mirror, mirror, on the wall, the back of the door, in my purse, or on either side of my car door, can I be the fairest of them all?

After reading what I just wrote I could spend a great deal of time on this issue of self-esteem. I believe this is where a great amount of exhausting time is spent talking to women trying to convince them what God says about them. Self-esteem is a tool the devil uses to keep you in bondage. It is a vehicle that keeps you from reaching the potential God has placed in you and it keeps you from performing the assignments God has given you to do. The most difficult thing to do is to change someone's mind about how they see and think about themselves. If you are going to succeed and overcome the ills that you feel have been placed on you because of your appearance or circumstances, you must believe what God says about you and not what other people say or have said about you, or what you think about yourself. No one is beyond changing how they think about themselves. No matter what people have said, no matter the circumstances you grew up in, no matter the education you received, no matter the peer pressure you faced or are facing, you can change if you want to. The one thing no one can take from you is the ability to choose. You have to choose to change how you think about yourself.

I remember at about the age of ten-years-old I realized I was shy. I was so withdrawn at an early age. And that thing stayed with me until I was well into my late twenties. There were many times I had to talk myself into just going to the store. But as I grew in Christ Jesus, I began to understand that this was one of the strongholds that would keep me from doing what God had called me to do. And, believe me, others saw it, and some people used my shyness to keep me in bondage. Even to this day I have encountered people who remind me of my shyness and say: "I can't believe it's you, a speaker. Hmm, you use to be so shy." Glory to God, for the power of the Holy Spirit living on the inside of me He delivered me from the fear of shyness. Often you will find your self-esteem issues keep you from exercising your spiritual gifts. The thing that keeps you in fear will prevent you from doing what God has called you to do. You have to change your mind about how you see yourself according to the Word of God.

Romans 12:2 says, *Do not conform any longer to the pattern of this world, but be transformed by the renewing of your mind.* When you believe what God says about you, you will have the power to change how you feel about yourself. It is no secret. Believe God and change your pattern of thinking. If you have felt this way about yourself all your life (you know what your stronghold has been, be honest with yourself), what or who has the power to change you from the way you think about yourself? I am sure you have tried to change and perhaps have hung your hopes on someone to help you change but without results. Look at what God says about you:

For you created my inmost being;
you knit me together in my mother's womb.
I praise you because I am fearfully and wonderfully made;
your works are wonderful,
I know that full well.
My frame was not hidden from you
when I was made in the secret place.
When I was woven together in the depths of the earth,
your eyes saw my unformed body.
All the days ordained for me
were written in your book
before one of them came to be.
Psalm 139:13-16 (New International Translation)

You made all the delicate, inner parts of my body
and knit me together in my mother's womb.
Thank you for making me so wonderfully complex!
Your workmanship is marvelous—how well I know it.
You watched me as I was being formed in utter seclusion,
as I was woven together in the dark of the womb.
You saw me before I was born.
Every day of my life was recorded in your book.
Psalm 139:13-16 (New Living Translation)

For You made the parts inside me.
You put me together inside my mother.
I will give thanks to You,
for the greatness of the way I was made brings fear.
Your works are great and my soul knows it very well.
My bones were not hidden from You
when I was made in secret and put together
with care in the deep part of the earth.
Your eyes saw me before I was put together.
And all the days of my life were written in
Your book before any of them came to be.
Psalm 139:13-16 (New Life Version)

Now exhale! I gave you three different translations to drive the point home in your heart. Do you believe what God has said about you? God created all your physical attributes whether you like them or not. There will always be something we don't like about them. Know this, there are no perfect bodies. Everyone has flaws on their body. We have gotten so caught up with the looks of women in the magazines and on television and we don't see their flaws because they are camouflaged.

As I was growing up I never understood why my feet were larger than my mom's and sisters'. They all wore sizes 6 and 7 shoes. I remember at the age of nine-years-old that I could fit into my mom's shoes. For a good while I had a big problem with the size of my feet because my feet continued to grow, and the comments others made certainly did not make me feel secure about them. I could not understand for the life of me why a 5'5" woman would have large feet. Not to mention that as I began to have children they kept growing. So, guess what? Now I wear a size 10 shoe. But for a very long time that was a difficult size to find in attractive women's shoes. Over the last 10 years or so I have been able to find fabulous shoes in a size 10. It wasn't until I understood that God created my feet to be a size 10 because He created me. I still don't understand all the reasons why, but I accepted the reality that I couldn't cut my feet in half. They were my feet and they were a size 10, and because God created them I fell in love with my feet. I thank God for my size 10 feet. Once I accepted the truth of God's Word about them and changed my thinking to agree with what God said, it freed me from poor self-esteem which had caused me to constantly try to hide my feet. Sis, I celebrate my feet now; they always have pretty shoes on them and the toenails stay polished. HA, HA!

Whatever physical attribute you struggle with, if you can change, it then do so, and stop allowing it to control and ruin your life. But if you cannot change it, then sis, you have to learn to accept it. You must change the way you think about yourself in light of what God says about you. Embrace you just as He has created you. *For you created my inmost being; you knit me together in my mother's womb.* Now all those other things that you *can* control, you can change if you want.

You have to stop allowing your current circumstances to define what you can be or what you can do. Are you making excuses not to move beyond your circumstances? I hear this all the time from women: I can't do this, I can't do that, I wish I could do this but…. You have too many excuses why you cannot do what God created you to do. Why can't you do it? What or who has so greatly influenced your life to cause you to think you do not have the capacity to achieve the, "*I can*"?

Sisters, we are good at this one. Stop! Right now make a list of all the things God is calling you to do and beside each one make a list of why you are not doing them. Surprise, Surprise! Now make a list of how you will accomplish those things God has called you to do. Philippians 1:6 says: *Being confident of this, that he who began a good work in you will carry it on to completion until the day of Christ Jesus.* The things that are in your heart, the desires that are pressing you, where do you think they came from?

I have concluded that I am not smart enough to concoct the things God has put in my heart to do. I don't possess the intellectual capabilities to invent ideas without God's divine intervention upon my heart and mind. Every time I respond to the pressing in my heart, it is a good work. When God put the desire in my heart to write the pilot to this book, I thought, What? Me? Write a book? But I tell you, it was pressing me. I know when God has put things in my heart as opposed to me placing them there. For me, it just presses me in my soul and no matter what I do it just will not go away. No one else can do those things God has given you to do but you. Begin setting goals to complete what God is calling you to do and do it. Stick to it; sometimes you give up to quickly. Stop convincing yourself you can't do the call.

Discouragement is the number one show stopper. And don't think because you have now set your heart to birth out your vision that you will not become discouraged. On the breath of every victory lies discouragement. Discouragement has two partners: Satan and people. Satan's job is to create an atmosphere that will cause you to have physiological issues when you are attaining the assignment God has given you. Before you know it, you are having doubts about God and doubting the assignment He has given you.

Satan will use people to discourage you with their words and their body language. Yes, body language. Have you ever shared your vision with someone and their eyes shift from side to side, they hem and haw, they get the deer stare in their eyes, their neck gets stiff, and you think for a moment you will have to give them CPR? People have a tendency to become jealous when God has given you an assignment they don't understand or they think should have been given to them. So in their quest to figure out what God is doing in your life, they will say things that can cause you to question what God has called you to do.

I have learned also with discouragement there are obstacles. You must define the obstacle. What is keeping me from accomplishing my goals? This is vital. When you define the obstacles you stop lying to yourself. Tell yourself the truth and face the obstacle. When you do this you will gain confidence, strength, and courage in accomplishing your goals. It is never too late and you are never too old to accomplish the assignment God has placed in your heart to do for His glory. It is time to move beyond what you think is impossible to the possible. You have the power. Now take another look in the mirror and see the new you. With God all things are possible.

Self Reflections/Group Discussion

1. Do you like what you see in the mirror? Why?

    _____

    _____

    _____

    _____

2. What excuses are you making not to do what God is calling you to do?

    _____

    _____

    _____

    _____

3. Study the list you made. Now set goals.

    _____

    _____

    _____

    _____

4. What are your obstacles of discouragement?

    _____

    _____

    _____

    _____

5. Everyday read Psalm 139:13-16 until you believe it.

    _____

    _____

    _____

    _____

5

*J*OINED AT THE HIP, DIET & EXERCISE

Ah, I just love food. I love how it tastes, I love how it feels in my mouth, and I love the smell of food. I just can't think of too many foods I don't like. I love cookies, cakes, pies, and there's nothing like hot bread and butter. I think about food all the time. Most days I plan at night what I will eat for breakfast, lunch, and dinner the next day. Then the rest of the day flows with junk foods. What is the first question you ask yourself when you are invited out for fellowship? I wonder what they are going to have to eat. Who's cooking the food? After eating everything you possibly can, do you ask for a doggie bag to take home to finish off later? Have you designed your life around food? Does this sound like you? Did you know God created our bodies to eat to live, and not live to eat? What love affair have you developed with food?

Every time I am with a group of women the topic of conversation begins with weight gain, diet and exercise. These concerns are discussed for the first hour of the gathering. Often I hear these statements: I don't know why I am gaining weight, I don't eat that much. I get home late and I eat at night. I eat all my food at lunch. I eat all my food at night because I am too busy in the daytime to eat. I eat all day long. I don't cook. It is only me so I eat out all my meals. I eat because my husband snacks at night. I don't have time to exercise. I am on medication. I am in menopause. Everyone in my family is big. I love this and that and just can't stop eating it. All the above are legitimate reasons for gaining weight. I play down none of them.

I have had my struggles all my life with eating and weight gain. I still have my struggles, but one thing I've learned is that diet and exercise goes hand in hand. You can't successfully do one without the other. I am not an advocate for skinny but I am an advocate for being healthy. Every time I eat I have to make a decision. I have the power to make a choice. That is the one thing I can do without permission from anyone. You have the power of choice every time you eat food. Who have you given your power of choice to? Think about it, every time you put food in your mouth you have to pick it up all by yourself, put it in your mouth and eat it. The power of choice is a gift from God. Every time you abuse the power of choice you offend God. 2 Peter 1:3 says: *His divine power has given us everything we need for life and godliness through our knowledge of Him who called us by His own glory and goodness.* Obesity has become a major epidemic in the world today.

I am not going to give you a diet plan but I am going to provoke your thinking and get you motivated in making changes about your love affair with food. There is too much information on the market today addressing healthy diet and exercise programs. It is no longer a mistake when you overindulge in eating; nor is any longer a mistake when you refuse to exercise. A mistake is made when you lack the information and are unaware of the consequences in making a decision. A choice is made when you have all the information and understand the consequences. Now you must conclude and be honest with yourself. You have been making choices. Every time I regained the weight I fought so desperately to lose, I asked myself, "How did I get back here again? Why do I keep making the same mistakes?" The Holy Spirit reminded me, "Iris, you are not making mistakes, you are making choices". You have all the information you need to overcome your overindulgences in eating. I worked so hard but yet I let my guard down, got comfortable with my old familiar way of eating. I made a choice to overindulge no matter the reason why I did it. I knew the consequences, yet I chose to overeat. It was not until I took ownership of my actions by being honest with me that I could change. No one is responsible for me gaining the weight but me. I have to make a choice every time I put food in my mouth. The will to choose is up to me.

Begin by identifying you. You have to be honest to yourself. You have to stop lying to yourself about your insatiable desire for food. You can begin any diet program you want but you will have no success if you are not honest with yourself. Tell yourself the truth. I love food because_____, I am out of control because_____. When you tell yourself the truth you take back your power from Satan and others. Right now, get a piece of paper and pen and write down why you love food. Read it. Mark 12:30 says, *Love the Lord your God with all your heart and with all your soul and with all your mind and with all your strength.* Now, go to God in prayer and seek His help and guidance. I am telling you, you cannot do it by yourself. If you could you would be successful by now. Only the Lord Jesus can break that uncontrollable desire for food. The object of your love has to shift from food to Jesus.

After you have identified you and are now honest with yourself, you need to develop a plan of action. You have to know you and your style of eating. Do I snack all day? Am I a late night eater? Do I skip meals and gorge at one meal? Do I eat junk foods all day? Do I eat too much at each meal? Do I eat because others are eating? How am I going to control my eating? Do I need help from a doctor or a structured program? On that same piece of paper identify your style of eating and if you will need help in achieving your goals. Remember diet and exercise go hand in hand.

I am an advocate for physical activity. Having been a former certified aerobics instructor for ten years and a leader for Weight Watchers group sessions, I know firsthand the importance and benefits of diet and exercise. Now that you have put your plan into action concerning your diet, you have to develop a plan of action for exercise. I have heard every excuse under the sun for why you can't exercise. I am too heavy. I don't like to sweat. I will mess up my hair. I will sweat out my perm. I don't have time. I can't afford to go to the gym. It is too much work. It makes my body too sore. I have small children and can't get out. My doctor told me not to exercise. What is your excuse for not getting exercise?

I have committed to some form of exercise everyday. Let me tell you, it is hard but I do it. There are no excuses for me except for being sick. Some days I kick and scream like a little child because I don't want to do it. It's hard work. If it could be done another way I would be the first to take it. I have developed a motto for myself to help me in exercising. "Don't think about it, just do it". I found there were times I would talk myself out of exercising. When you make the commitment to exercise it cannot be based on other people. If you team up with a friend and they decide they're not going to exercise today, will you? I never based my exercise routine around anyone. I have exercised with friends but my commitment was for me. If they decided they were not going today, I went anyway. I learned it is better to go solo, and then there are no excuses to make for not exercising. But, if you really need support to motivate you, there are several options to choose from. A membership at a local gym is very stimulating, aerobic classes; adequate aerobics and personal trainer are food for thought. My commitment is not based on another person's performance and yours should not be either. Exercise has to become a discipline of life.

The word *discipline* means: *control gained by enforcing obedience or order, orderly or prescribed conduct or pattern of behavior, SELF–control.* Now it has to become self-discipline for success. You will have to discipline yourself because no one can exercise for you. This discipline is going to require you to make time, be committed, and be consistent. Self-discipline will do away with the excuses. Self-discipline has to be in alignment with wisdom. How will I discipline myself to exercise? How will I stay committed and be consistent in exercising? James 1:5 says, *If any of you lacks wisdom, he should ask God, who gives generously to all without finding fault, and it will be given to him.*

Making time for exercise can be a challenge. It is your responsibility to locate times in your day that you can allocate to exercise. If you take a long look at your day you will find holes, as I call them that you can use for exercise. What about your lunch break at work? What about when the children are taking a nap? When you are chilling? Oh, maybe we need to take a break here. Perhaps, you are just lazy. Could that be it? Have you just become so complacent in your couch potato state that you're just lazy? It is okay; you can change your mind right now about being lazy. It is your choice! Identify holes in your day that you can commit to exercise.

How will I stay consistent? Consistency is the key. If you can only exercise a little each day, then do it. If you can only exercise a few days a week, then do it. Whatever schedule you develop to begin an exercise program just stick to it. Ask yourself, what form of exercise will I do? Most of you have some form of exercise equipment sitting in its designated corner collecting dust, holding clothes or collecting cobwebs, just waiting for a chance to be used for the purpose it was designed for and the purpose you purchased it for. Let the church say Amen! You can start right there with what you have. Choose exercises that will fit your specific goals. Now, what are your goals? Are you exercising to lose weight? Are you exercising to increase your stamina? Are you exercising to increase muscle? Begin to identify your goals. After you have identified your goals, how will you get started? Will I join a gym? Will I purchase exercise equipment? Will I need to get medical advice from my doctor? Will I walk? Will I swim? You have to determine what form of exercise is best for you, but whatever you decide, don't give up. It takes time and consistency before you see results. Be realistic about your goals. Start small. You have to take control of your health.

The benefits of exercising will strengthen your heart, increase blood flow, reduce high cholesterol, increase endurance, burns calories, release good endorphins and is proven to enhance the quality of your life.

Now that you are honest with yourself and you're thinking of a plan of action, your success will be determined by your commitment to that plan. The word *commitment* according to the dictionary means: *an agreement or pledge to do something, the state or an instance of being obligated or emotionally impelled.* Are you ready to commit to your plan of action? Can you be trusted to make an agreement with God and yourself? Have you come to a state of being emotionally impelled to becoming a healthier you? Commitment is going to cost you perhaps some discomfort, some self-denial, and some tears. Your days are numbered by God, you cannot change this, but you can live the very best you by incorporating an exercise plan in your life. It is in these moments God will show Himself mighty on your behalf if you let Him. Are you ready to eat to live and stop living to eat? Are you ready to incorporate a healthy diet and exercise program in your life? Proverbs 16:3 says: *Commit to the Lord whatever you do, and your plans will succeed.*

Self Reflections/Group Discussion

1. Am I having a love affair with food? Why?

_____

_____

_____

_____

2. Am I out of control in my eating?

_____

_____

_____

_____

3. What changes do I need to make to become healthy?

_____

_____

_____

_____

4. Do I need medical help? Why?

_____

_____

_____

_____

5. Develop a plan of action.

_____

_____

_____

_____

6

*S*KIN *DEEP*

emember the song, *Beauty's Only Skin Deep, yeah, yeah, yeah*. Well, it's true. Our skin is the outer covering of our body. Think about it for a moment. I define the skin as the outer shell of the nostrils. Just as the nose is needed to breathe air in and out of the body, so the skin needs to breathe to be healthy. The condition of our skin tells the story of how we take care of it. Our skin is one of the most exceptional gifts from God. Although our skin tone comes in all varieties, yet no two are alike. I have discovered during various group discussions with women of various ages that most women feel guilty about making time to care for their skin. I have also discovered that the guilt range expands as far as including regular doctor's appointments, hair care, manicures, pedicures, massages, facials, and just putting lotion or Vaseline on dry skin after a bath or shower. It is important to take the very best care of your skin as possible. We are going to talk about each one of these vital areas. Hey, if the shoe fits take it off and soak your feet, relax and continue reading.

There is a very interesting woman in the Bible and I love her, her name is Esther. We can learn a lot from her. Esther 2:12-13 says, *Before a girl's turn came to go in to King Xerxes, she had to complete twelve months of beauty treatments prescribed for the women, six months with oil of myrrh and six with perfumes and cosmetics.*

And this is how she would go to the king. Now you know Esther was not accustomed to beauty treatments. She was an orphaned Israelite girl from the tribe of Benjamin and lived with her cousin Mordecai. Esther 2:7: *Mordecai had a cousin named Hadassah, whom he had brought up because she had neither father nor mother. This girl, who was also known as Esther, was lovely in form and features, and Mordecai had taken her as his own daughter when her father and mother died.*

After Esther got over the shock of being taken from her home to the king's palace to possibly become the king's queen, can you imagine Esther's bliss when she found out that she was going to receive twelve months of beauty treatments? All of this was new for Esther. Remember she was being prepared to meet the king so her beauty treatments were consistent for twelve months. It took time. You have to begin to schedule time for body treatments.

Massages are one of the very best treatments for stress release, tension, relaxation and skin softening. Also, massages stimulate the lymphatic system, relieve sore achy muscles, and after you have indulged in one you will understand the importance of having a massage. A professional massage is a must try. I have friends who have never had a professional massage. There are many excuses: I am too fat nobody wants to rub on me, they may want to charge me more because I am heavy, I don't like strangers rubbing on me, girl, I am not spending money on that, and on and on. They are not super expensive; however, if your budget is stressed there are options. Hand-held massagers, neck massagers, and chair pad massagers work very well. But you must make time for the experience.

Esther had six months of treatments with oil. Now whether the oil was rubbed on her body or she soaked in it, she felt worthy, energized and relaxed. Another great skin care regiment is soaking in the tub. There are so many new and improved products on the market that aid the skin. I love Epsom salt soaks along with a skin softener. I hear you, you have small children and a job and you are just too tired in the evening for this simple pleasure. Well, you can't continue to afford not to. You can find fifteen minutes to get in the tub. There is a two-fold blessing: your skin gets nourished and you release some stress and taking a soak in a hot tub of Epsom salt can truly do the trick.

Surely, Esther could not enter the king's presence stressed out because if she did all she would have talked about was the drama of her stressed-out life. "You know, king, they got on my last nerve on the job today, oh, I know she was tripping today. Let me tell you what she said to me. Lucky, I'm a Christian, king, the kids tore my house down today, and I'm ready to put them all away. Oh, king, what should I do? All my bills are overdue". Um-hm, you are all stressed out.

The first thing the king was going to see was Esther's face. Esther was not accustomed to getting facials; she was probably a splash girl. She probably got up in the morning and splashed some water on her face. During her beauty treatments she was getting facials. Zits, blackheads, whiteheads, pimples, and bags were not going to win favor with the king. You can get a professional facial and they will teach you how to properly care for your skin and then you can learn to do it yourself. Do some research and develop a regiment that will work for you. It is time to move away from the old splash some water on my face and go. Granted, we are all going to wrinkle, some more than others, but we can do it with grace by just applying some techniques with the right products for results that will keep your face healthy and glowing.

Now when Esther was going to meet the king, she did not know if he was going to kiss her hand to greet her. Can you see her tips half-off, fingers with bandages on, and her polish chipped? Sisters, manicures are essential. If you are going to wear tips keep them current. Make the time to go for the two-week appointment. Don't wait till they start falling off and look tacky. If you can't keep them up it is just better to go with a clear nail polish with a clear top-coat or polish them yourself. If you are not interested in spending the money, do it yourself. Just make time to do it.

During Esther's time they wore sandals. The women had the same toes like we have. The same toenails we have. Now when Esther was being prepared during her beauty treatments, you know she had to get pedicures. Just imagine when she was dressing to impress she probably had picked beautiful jeweled sandals. Sandals like she never had before. Can you imagine her toenails all jacked up and scaly bottom feet? I don't care how ugly you think your feet are they deserve attention. A professional pedicure can do for your toes and the bottom of your feet what you cannot do. You get to sit still and soak your feet in hot water. The chair in most nail salons is a massage chair so that is a double treat. Your toenails get cleaned out and you would be surprised at the junk that gets imbedded in your toenails. All that scaly stuff gets cleaned off the bottom of your feet. The Pedicurist gives you a foot and leg massage and the puts lotion on them, heck, just getting the leg and foot massage is worth going. Then you get your toes polished in a beautiful color of your choice or you can take your own polish. That right there is like new money. Trust me. You are worth it and your feet will thank you. Hey, don't give me that excuse, "Well no one is going see my feet anyway". You will and, truthfully, it isn't about anyone else.

Esther's hair was right. Those handmaidens were taking care of her all day bathing her and washing her hair. They probably experimented with different hairstyles that would suit her entrance in meeting the king. I don't think I have too much to say about the hair. I know of some women who would rather be hungry then to have jacked-up hair. Guess what? I am one of them. There is no reason not to take care of your hair. If your hair is giving you problems, deal with it. My hair started to thin in my 40s. Stress, aging and, I am sure, other things I had done to my hair over the years played a part, but you know what? I have two best friends: Wig and Weave. Step outside your narrow box and try it. Just want to encourage you if you get perms and you can't afford a touch up when it is time for one; you need to have an alternative. You know why? You are worth it.

If Esther was positioning herself for the queen's position she could not enter into the king's presence sick. I am sure they had ways of dealing with certain illnesses. Why do you hate to go to the doctor? There are some appointments that are absolutely necessary: mammogram screening, pap smears, colon screening, heart screening, bone density testing, blood testing, high blood pressure testing, cholesterol testing and diabetes testing. This is the only body you have and God expects you to take care of it. Women are dying everyday from things that could be prevented if they had just taken the time and visited a doctor. If these things are caught early through the proper testing they can be treated. Many women are living a poor quality of life because they waited too long before they visited the doctor. And what is so sad about this is that most women have some form of health insurance. But if you choose to blame your lack of interest in visiting the doctor on not having health insurance, there are many times during the year when you can get free screening and help. If you have neglected your health care, make time and make a change. Go to the phone and make an appointment. Stop living in the dark, guessing, and trying to diagnose your self. You are worth.

The twelve months of Esther's treatments were broken into six months. The first six months was with myrrh oil and the next six months was with perfume and cosmetics. We all know what perfume is. It is that sweet smell that distinguishes you from others. Some women call it their signature fragrance. Remember, if a perfume smells good on someone it may not smell the same on you. Everyone has different body chemistry. Experiment and find a fragrance that works for you. Cosmetics are designed to help our complexion and enhance our attractiveness. Makeup is okay. A little dab won't hurt you. If you are not sure how to apply it or what you need, go to the mall and check out the cosmetic counters. They have professionally trained staff who will give you a makeup makeover—sometimes free. Don't be afraid to try something new. If you don't like it go home and wash it off. During Esther's six months of perfume and cosmetics they taught her how to wear makeup.

I must pause and address one other important issue because Esther did not meet the king naked. You have heard the old cliché, "Clothes don't make a woman, but the woman makes the clothes". This is true. One woman can have on a $500.00 designer outfit and another woman can have on a $15.00 Wal-Mart outfit. The emphasis is not on the cost of the outfit but the confidence one has on the inside wearing the outfit. Dressing starts on the inside. You have also heard, "First impression is a lasting impression". It is okay to look nice in your clothing. You should want to look nice, not for others, but for yourself. Learn your body type and dress appropriately. Just because it is the current style doesn't mean it was meant for you and just because you like it doesn't constitute you wearing it. If it is hard for you to decide what looks good on you, find a friend you can trust to tell you the truth. Take her shopping with you to be your second mirror.

Understanding Esther's modest background and her opportunity to wear anything that would entice the king to choose her, she probably kept it sharp but simple. When she entered the king's presence he saw her, not her clothes, and that is the art of apparel.

We can conclude that Esther's preparation for her entrance to meet the king was successful because she became Queen Esther. Let's thank God for leaving us a testimony of the importance of taking care of ourselves. Stop for a moment and exhale. Now have you been too busy to incorporate the care you so desperately need and deserve? Perhaps now is the time to make a list of the areas you have neglected and make a commitment to change. Don't allow guilt to prevent you from taking care of yourself. There is nothing to feel guilty about. These are just a few things you have placed on the back burner and forgotten about because you are too busy, tired, depressed, don't think it matters, or suppressed by someone else. Get your fire back. Start to incorporate something you just read. Make a promise to stop neglecting you. Don't forget the little things that remind you that you are a woman created by God.

Self Reflections/Group Discussion

1. When was your last doctor's appointment? Why?

   _____

   _____

   _____

   _____

2. I am making a commitment to see the doctor on _____.

   _____

   _____

   _____

   _____

3. What have you wanted to try but was afraid of others' opinions?

   _____

   _____

   _____

   _____

4. Which Esther treatment will you begin today?

   _____

   _____

   _____

   _____

5. Look at your wardrobe. Do you need to make any changes? Discuss dressing from the inside out.

   _____

   _____

   _____

   _____

7

ME ON A BUDGET? PLEASE

Yes, you on a budget. This is not the time to close this book. God did it again! He backed me into a corner and said, "Write it". Again I struggled with this topic because no one likes to spend money more than I do. Perhaps you? Who wants to be on a budget? But it is necessary to begin to look at where you are spending your money and what you are spending it on. Granted, you may not have a problem with being on a budget. You may be one of the special women who never, ever waste a penny. You never purchase anything that is not on the list. If that is you, kudos to you! Everyone give her a hand because she deserves it. Now for the rest of us who woke up this morning and thought, "This could be my last day on earth", and if I don't buy it for myself, no one is going to buy it for me. So what do I want to buy today? Or you went to lunch and just happened to glance in the window and saw those beautiful shoes and decided to take a closer look at them. Now you are in the store trying on the shoes and the store clerk informs you that they have only one pair left in your size. You think, how can I not purchase these? They will be gone if I wait till I get paid. Now you are putting the shoes in the trunk of your car because you had to have them. Later conviction begins to set in and you tell yourself, "Well, I will pay that bill off by the end of the month." If you can afford to buy the shoes then justify it. It's all good. But if you can't afford to buy the shoes keep reading. It is time to examine what you are spending your money on and why. There are three major spending epidemics in our society today: keeping up with thy neighbor, credit cards and emotional voids.

Do you feel pressure to keep up with thy neighbor? Often this happens. Years ago they called it keeping up with the Jones's. The reasoning is this: "Well, if they can get it so can I. They are no better than I am. If it is good enough for them, well, it is better for me." It doesn't matter what it is: homes, cars, clothes, jewelry, appliances, furniture or electronics, this type of reasoning is a trap. Once you develop this attitude of thinking, you will find yourself in competition to keep up with thy neighbor. Not to mention the pressure put on parents to keep their children current in the latest styles because of peer pressure. There is nothing wrong at all with having things. I love nice things and I know you do to. God gives us things. They are blessings from Him. I believe God desires to give us the best. Remember what God said in Deuteronomy 29:9 *Carefully follow the terms of this covenant, so that you may prosper in everything you do.*

But through experience and wisdom I know God doesn't want us to covet what our neighbor has. Exodus 20:17 says, *You shall not covet your neighbor's house. You shall not covet your neighbor's wife, or his manservant or maidservant, his ox or donkey, or anything that belongs to your neighbor.* The definition for the word, *covet* according to the dictionary is: *to wish for enviously, to desire (what belongs to another) inordinately or culpably.* I want to take a quick pause while we are here to say this: Stop wanting her husband. Stop wishing, "if only he was my husband". He is not! That's right, you heard the old saying, "The grass always looks greener on the other side and everything that glitters isn't gold". You never know how your neighbor acquired what they have. But you will find yourself in debt because you wanted it and just had to have it now.

There is a price to pay for having it now if you don't pay cash for it, it is called interest rate. If you took a survey you would not find many women who don't have one credit card or more with a balance of at least $500.00. But on a real note, many women owe more like $10,000.00 or more on the credit card. The interest rates alone will keep you paying on credit cards for a very long time. Interest rates for credit cards range from 7% to 30% and in some cases higher. Don't get mad at me. I want to provoke your thinking about how you are spending your money and if you don't like how you are spending your money than make a change. It is so easy to use a credit card. It provides immediate gratification. You saw what you wanted, signed your name and took your purchase. When the bills come, you ask yourself, "When and why did I buy this?" Five years from now you are still paying the bill and cannot trace where the items are. Oh, yes, they are bagged up in chapter seven, funny. Not to mention the fee for insufficient funds on that debt card because you failed to keep your checkbook balanced. You assumed you had money in the checking account, made your purchase, only to find you were short one dollar and therefore you must pay the bank thirty or thirty-five dollars for being a dollar short. You just gave away money because you failed to take responsibility for how you handled your money.

Budgeting is not easy for everyone. Take another survey and you will find that most women don't know how to balance their checkbook or refuse to take the time to learn. Are you paying the bank bounced charge fees every month? What about paying your bills on time? Oh, girl, this month I am going to rob Peter to pay Paul. Have you used that one before? And you know what; you rob God to pay Paul. How many times have you spent your tithes and offerings? Yes, in tithes and offerings. Malachi 3:8 says: *"Will a man rob God? Yet you rob me. But you ask, 'How do we rob you?'" "In tithes and offerings."* Okay, this is your first responsibility with your money to give back to God what He requires in tithes and offerings. Look at what God says: Haggai 1:5-11, *Now this is what the LORD Almighty says: "Give careful thought to your ways. You have planted much, but have harvested little. You eat, but never have enough. You drink, but never have your fill. You put on clothes, but are not warm. You earn wages, only to put them in a purse with holes in it." This is what the LORD Almighty says: "Give careful thought to your ways. Go up into the mountains and bring down timber and build the house, so that I may take pleasure in it and be honored," says the LORD. "You expected much, but see, it turned out to be little. What you brought home, I blew away. Why?" declares the LORD Almighty. "Because of my house, which remains a ruin, while each of you is busy with his own house. Therefore, because of you the heavens have withheld their dew and the earth its crops. I called for a drought on the fields and the mountains, on the grain, the new wine, the oil and whatever the ground produces, on men and cattle, and on the labor of your hands."* Listen, it is time to make a change.

And then there are those of us who spend money out of control because there is a void we are trying to fill. Been there, done that. There are many things we use to fill voids in our lives, this is just one. Know that buying things only makes you feel good for the moment. Voids are empty spaces that yearn to be filled. We can learn a lesson from Leah when it comes to filling a void in our life.

Leah was desperate to be loved by her husband Jacob. So she believed if she gave him children that he would love her. She bore seven children and attached a significant meaning to each of their names based upon where she was in her thinking, her rationale, and her emotions, which all were instrumental in her trying to fill her void to be loved. The children's names were as follows:

> Reuben - See a son. Now he will love me. (Genesis 29:32)
> Simeon - Heard. God has heard. I am not loved. (Genesis 29:33)
> Levi - Attached. Now he will become attached to me.
> (Genesis 29:34)
> Judah - Praise. She turns her eyes to the Lord. (Genesis 29:35)

After Leah has given birth to four children God shuts her womb up and Leah loses her focus. She believes she has lost her leverage in her attempts to make her husband love her. She sends her maidservant Zilpah to her husband and she births two children for Leah.

> Gad - Good fortune. (Genesis 30:10)
> Asher - How happy am I. The women will call me happy.
> (Genesis 30:12)
> Now, God opens Leah's womb and she births:
> Issachar - God rewarded me for giving my maidservant to
> Jacob. (Genesis 30:18)

Zebulun - Precious gift. This time Jacob will honor me.
(Genesis 30:20)
Dinah - Justice. Balance. (Genesis 30:21)

Leah's attempts to fill her void blinded her to embrace who really loved her. God expressed His love to Leah by allowing her the privilege to birth children. Leah gave birth to 8 of the 12 tribes of Judah. Upon the birth of her last child perhaps she got it—balance. This is the place you have to come to with emotions. Stop trying to fill the voids in your life with things and allow the Lord to fill that space first with His love. Read Romans, chapter 5.

If you need help in preparing a budget there are free resources that will help you get your finances on track. Don't allow pride to keep you from admitting you are in trouble and need help with your finances. You have the capacity and are capable of being on a budget and keeping balance in your spending. Get out of the loop of self-gratification and ignorance and begin to take responsibility for your spending. It is time to take inventory of your finances and learn how to become diligent in handling the money God has blessed you with. Amen and praise God.

Self Reflections/Group Discussion

1. What part of this chapter can you identify with?

2. Discuss Leah. How can you relate to her?

3. Read Malachi 3:8 and Haggai 1:5-11. How did this impact you?

4. Discuss peer pressure and the parenting.

5. What changes will you make in your budget?

8

CLEAN IT UP AND LET IT GO

*I*cringed when I wrote this title. Do what? Clean it up and
let it go. Clean up? I thought, my house is not dirty. No, it is
not, but be very careful when you open up the hidden areas.
Surprise, Surprise, Surprise. Be real with me for a moment, sisters.
Alright, perhaps you don't want to go there, so I will use myself as
an example and gently pull you in. I understand it is a touchy topic.
I have so much stuff it is ridiculous. I could have two of something
and before I give you one I would rather go purchase you the same
thing. Have you ever gone shopping for someone's birthday gift or
Christmas gift and when you got back home you said, "Oh, I can't
give her this; it is so pretty and it looks so good on me. I'll have
to go back to the store tomorrow and buy her another gift." Um-
hm, I know guilty, me too. Have you ever actually given someone
something and regretted it after you gave it to them? Um-hm, I
know guilty, me too. What about that outfit you gave away and
saw the sister in it and had to give her a compliment on the outfit
that you wished you had not given away? Um-hm, I know guilty,
me too. Here are some of my favorite words: I wish I had kept that.
Why did I give that away? I must have had a moment of weakness.
Have you ever had so much remorse after giving something away

you cried? Um-hm, I know guilty, me too. Woe, let's stop right now and laugh at ourselves. Ha, ha, ha, ha, ha.

I took a good long look at my closet and decided I would start there. Perhaps this would be a good place for you to start also. As I began to count the endless pairs of shoes I had, I got tired of counting. Sometimes you have to understand why you do what you do in order to be delivered from what you do. Why so many shoes, Iris? I asked myself. Because I grew up in poverty, I had a thing for shoes. Oh my goodness, I will buy shoes before I have the outfit to go with them. I have bought shoes that were pretty just to have them in my collection of shoes. Shoes, clothes, purses, coats, and lingerie, I have overindulged for years. The sad part of this picture is my lack of ability to let go of things I am not wearing. It was painful to pull out clothes and throw them in a pile after reminiscing over how much I paid for each item, what I wore it to, how good I looked in it, couldn't fit into it anymore, but maybe one day I would be able to wear it again. It was difficult to give away shoes I no longer wore and purses I no longer used. I don't even want to talk about the panties, bras, and stocking drawers. I cannot begin to tell you how many different sizes, styles, and colors, I have tried that did not work but they were still taking up needed space in the drawer. Just let them go. Right then the Holy Spirit convicted me about holding on.

Here is the problem. We tend to hold on so tight to things. Not only do we hold on tight to things but just about everything. We tend to hold on to hurts, bad memories, bad relationships, unpleasant experiences, sicknesses and things that just don't work for us. Why do we do this? Because when we make a connection to something it becomes a part of our being. We have a strong sense of commitment; it is coded in our DNA. If it is broken I will fix it. If it is not working I will wait. I will never advance in this job but I am working. I am sick so I will stay sick. They treat me badly but they are my friends. There comes a time when you have to let go of things and people. You will make yourself crazy trying to hold on and fix what cannot be fixed.

Holding on to things will begin to choke you and that's what was happening to me. I felt suffocated when I looked around my home, in the closets, the drawers, the cabinets, and the office. I felt suffocated when I looked at the people in my life I was holding on to, and I felt suffocated in my heart with the things I was holding onto. It was time to clean it up and let it go. Be aware that this abundance of things in life isn't equal to the abundance in our relationship with Jesus. We have to begin now to overflow in abundance of relationship with Jesus and whatever is blocking that from happening has to go.

Clothes I had not worn last season and those that did not fit, whether too big or too small, went in the pile on the floor. I made a vow with God and myself that once it hit the floor I could not pick it up again. Some items still had the price tag. How sad. But, you know, I am not alone. It was difficult but I did it. Here are some thoughts: What if God wants to bless you with something else but you have no room to receive it? What if God wants to bless you with good memories? What if God wants to bless you with good relationships? What if God desires to bless you with a new job position? What if God desires to heal you? What if God wants to fix the broken? What if? How would you ever know if you are not willing to let go of the things that are suffocating you? Now, what are you going to do with your closet? It is time to clean it up and let it go.

Let's talk about other items in the home, such as knickknacks and trinkets, as they are called. Some of you have so many little things all over your tables, in corners, in cabinets, from way back on the other side of years ago. Every time a family member or friend went on vacation they brought you back a souvenir and you have held onto it because you feel guilty getting rid of it. Perhaps you started a collection and now it is overflowing and you have no more room. Pack them up and store them or give them away. It's okay, I feel your pain. You can change your attitude about life by cleaning up your environment. What about all those pictures of your family all over the walls and tables. Oh, it's good to have pictures of the family around. I have them, but I want you to look at them for a minute. Are they hung crooked on the wall? Are the frames tarnished and worn? Are the pictures faded? Take a minute and revive the pictures. Perhaps now that your children are 20ish and 30ish the baby pictures can go into a photo album and current pictures can be displayed.

What about all that china, crystal glasses, and polished silverware that is hidden away and never used. This is what I here sisters say, "Oh, I only use the china, crystal and silverware on special occasions". But guess what? You never have special occasions. It serves as decoration and now it has become clutter. Guess what? Use it or get rid of it. Everyday you eat off of the same old dinky plastic plates, cracked and chipped, drink out of the same old plastic glasses and eat off that tarnished old bent-up silverware. Girl, take the china, the polished silverware, and the crystal glasses out of the cabinet and use them tonight. Make today a special occasion and everyday after this. It's okay. It is not going to get broken and if it does, so what? Use it. Enjoy what you have right now. Life is short and you are not going to live forever on this earth, so start making every meal a special occasion.

How about all those books, magazines, old bills, newspapers, price tags, receipts, old phone books, and junk mail, that take up space and have no use whatsoever? You have books that belonged to your children when they were children collecting dust. Why not donate them to the Goodwill store?

Magazines are wonderful. I love magazines but they can accumulate so fast that before you know it you have stacks upon stacks of magazines. It is hard to part with magazines you have paid for and there is always an article you want to keep. I gathered all the magazines I had and cut the articles out that were of importance to me, placed them in a folder, then scanned them into my computer and burned them on a disk. The disks are easy to store and take up little room. I then passed on the magazine.

I think everyone has a box of old bills. When I looked into that box designated for paid bills I wanted to scream. I had paid bills dating back to 1985. What is wrong with me? I thought. All the old bills got bagged up for the shredder. I am only keeping two years of bills. I was able to free so much space that is now just empty. I know you don't want to go through all that stuff, but you have to. Clean it up and let it go. Just do it.

Oh, I love this one old newspaper. Let's examine this one. I used to get the daily paper and the Sunday paper. Before I knew it I had stacks of paper. I thought, what do we use newspaper for? Well, growing up if you ran out of toilet paper you got out the newspaper. Funny, funny, funny, but it is true. If you were training your puppy you used the newspaper on the floor to catch the mistakes the puppy made and then you used newspaper to beat him if he missed the paper again. If the sink, tub, toilet, dishwasher, or washing machine ran over you would scream, "Somebody get some newspaper". Crab lovers, get the newspaper. When you changed the baby's pamper you got the newspaper to wrap it up. And if by chance you ran out of newspaper you called your girlfriend and asked her to bring you some. You would not believe how much newspaper some people have. I got rid of all that newspaper. Although we have explored and discovered the many uses for newspaper, there is no reason to keep stacks upon stacks of them. I only keep the Sunday newspaper. Clean it up and let it go. Just do it.

Every time I make a purchase I get a receipt and a price tag. When I make a purchase and get a receipt, the receipt goes into my wallet and the price tag into a drawer because I may have to return the item for some reason unknown to me at the time. We all save our receipts. Here is my problem: When my wallet gets too fat with receipts, I transfer them to a Ziploc bag for easy storage and throw the price tag into the drawer. But when I have accumulated bags upon bags and tags upon tags from years and years, it is now a problem. I thought, after thirty days the receipt is invalid most of the time with the exception of stores that give you ninety days. So, I got rid of all those receipts and cleaned out the drawer of tags and kept one bag that gets cleaned out once a month. Wherever you keep all those store receipts and tags, clean them up and let them go. Just do it.

Old phone books are the worst. They are so big and it was just easy for me to stack them. After awhile there was a big stack. I carried them to the recycle bin—most supermarkets have one. Toss the junk mail. What a waste of time and money and while you are at it, clean up the emails. Clean it up and let it go. Just do it.

This may have been a difficult chapter for you to read if you are known as a pack rat. Simply meaning, you have a very hard time throwing away things. It is okay, but be honest with yourself. Here is a good test for a pack rat. When you pick up the item you want to get rid of, how does it make you feel? Can you live without it? Is it enhancing your life? Would be any better or worse if you got rid of it? Could you be a blessing to someone if you gave it away? Take a minute and do self-examination.

After accumulating things and holding on to them over the years, it has been exciting and liberating to clean them up and let them go. If you are there, here is your opportunity to make a change. God desires to do new things in your life. Clean it up and let it go. Just do it.

Mark 2:22 says: *And no one pours new wine into old wineskins. If he does, the wine will burst the skins, and both the wine and the wineskins will be ruined. No, he pours new wine into new wineskins.*

Self Reflections/Group Discussion

1. What am I holding on to? Why

    _____

    _____

    _____

    _____

2. Where will I start cleaning out?

    _____

    _____

    _____

    _____

3. I am ready to make a donation to an organization. Which one?

    _____

    _____

    _____

    _____

4. What does Mark 2:22 say to me?

    _____

    _____

    _____

    _____

5. Pray a prayer of renewal and cleansing.

    _____

    _____

    _____

9

ME TIME

Mark 6:30-31 says, *The apostles gathered around Jesus and reported to him all they had done and taught. Then, because so many people were coming and going that they did not even have a chance to eat, he said to them, "Come with me by yourselves to a quiet place and get some rest."*

Me time sounds pretty selfish, right! Well, it is. It is exactly that. It is time you designate to retreat, replenish, rejuvenate, and rest. No matter how important you think your are, no matter how much you have on your plate, no matter if you think no one else can do it like you can or as good as you can, no matter if you have a house full of children or you have no children, no matter if you are married or not married, none of this matters. You have neglected yourself for a long time meeting the demands of life, and now you are in desperate need of me time. As we talk about me time you may begin to feel guilty about giving yourself undivided attention that is well needed. In various conversations I have had with women this topic always strikes a nerve and that's okay. Let's define me time. Perhaps this will give you a starting point in grasping this concept.

Me time is time I designate to myself within the day or on a specific day to retreat, replenish, rejuvenate, and rest myself.

Now you may be thinking why do I need to do this? You just don't know what a day in my life holds. I can't find time to do what

I am already doing. This is exactly why me time is necessary for you. You are coming apart at the seams because the demands of your life are kicking your butt. There are times when you feel like you are hyperventilating, or perhaps you are, your heart is racing, you're irritable, you're tired, you're borderline depressed, you're confused, you're experiencing all types of medical problems and, you wonder why. You will not be able to continue to function at your greatest capacity if you do not begin to ascribe me time.

I invited a few of my friends to tea one day and they were so elated about stopping to have a cup of tea in the hustle and bustle of their day. What was interesting to me was a comment one of my friends made. She said, "This is wonderful. When I retire this is one of the things I will be doing". I thought to myself, and then I said to her, "Why wait until you retire to enjoy such a simple pleasure?" After she thought about my comment for a minute, she said, "You know, you are right. But I will have more time after I retire". There will never be enough time in your day if you are waiting to find me time. Your decision in making me time cannot be based on after this happens or before that happens. You have to honestly evaluate your day and take me time.

Me time has to become just as important as the other tasks you carry out in your day. Jesus said to the apostles, "*Come with me*". He extends an invitation to them to retreat. If you are going to become successful in incorporating me time you must give yourself permission to do so. Oftentimes we retreat when we have played our last chord or after someone has gotten on our last nerve. I can remember when I would wait so long to retreat away from home for a week to rest and I would say to myself, I will never wait this long again to get away, only to return and find myself in that same place again. Once I changed my thinking about carving time out of the day just for me, I am able to actually enjoy myself even more so when I go away for a vacation because I am not taking all that woe is me, I am so tired drama with me. After fulfilling your daily responsibilities you become depleted and need to find ways to retreat everyday.

Me time is necessary to replenish yourself. *Replenish* means: *to fill and build up again*. There are days when you have given so much of yourself away to everything and everyone else's expectations that you are just drained. What areas do you need to replenish? What has become empty? What has become broken down and needs to be built up again? Ask yourself these questions. After you identify these areas you will be able to decide what you need to do to replenish yourself.

There have been times in my life when I have been so busy and so drained that sitting down to eat a good meal was not an option. I would eat on the run, most often in the car. As I got older I realized the importance of just sitting down and eating a healthy meal to gain strength and energy to carry on. After a good meal I felt replenished because I made time to sit down and eat. Now read Mark 6:39 after the apostles went with Jesus to a quiet place (I am sure the first thing on the agenda for the apostles was to eat because they were hungry), which turned out not to be so quiet after the crowds began to follow them. But even in the midst of the distraction He continued to teach the hungry people.

Maybe you are just void of food and it has caused a chain reaction. The average person is irritable and tired when they are hungry. Now, that is the truth, the whole truth, and nothing but the truth. That is the first thing I ask a person when they are showing signs of irritability, "When was the last time you ate"? This is a good place to start. Sit yourself down and have a good meal today.

Me time allows you to rejuvenate yourself. *Rejuvenate* means: *to stimulate; to restore to original or new state.* When was the last time you had a new idea? Remember the things you used to enjoy doing? Why have you stopped doing them? Is there something you have always wanted to do but never did it? Where is your creativity? Have you lost it? You have forgotten the joy in experiencing and exploring a new idea. You're too busy and you say there is no time. I have heard people in conversation say, "I miss doing this and that." Then I have friends who say, "You know, I have five or six weeks of vacation that I can carry over to this next year". I think, for what? Why are you so concerned about carry-over vacation time? The purpose of having vacation time is to come out of the familiar environment and do something you miss doing. Help me out. Do people in the workplace brag, or is it a social status among employees to think they have accomplished such a great thing as to carry over vacation time? Please! Every job I had, I made sure I used ever bit of my vacation time when I earned it. Save it, for what purpose? I would take me days and you should too. During times of rejuvenation you get back in tune with yourself.

These are the times you notice things about your body that you may have been missing. You begin to quiet your mind and hear something other than noise. Jesus said to the apostles in Mark 6:31, *"Come with me by yourselves to a quiet place"*. They were asked to come alone. Go by yourself and be alone. In the solitude of space you can rediscover you. In this space you can regain your creativity, your focus, and your vigor for life.

Me time allows you to rest. *Rest is the freedom from activity or labor; motionless.* I often hear people say, "Rest for what? I will rest when I die." Well, you are right about that. At the rate you are going it could be sooner than you think. Rest is to the body like food is to the stomach; you can go only so long without it. Jesus instructed the apostles, *get some rest*. Sister, get some rest. Many women are suffering from sleep depravation. You stay up all hours of the night and you get up early in the morning. By midday you are exhausted. You're sleepy. Reset your clock. Rest is not only sleeping but being still. When was the last time you just sat? Um-hm. Did you know it is hard for some women to be still? I use to be hyperactive. I felt I had to spend every minute of the day and evening doing something. As I got older and began to understand the importance of rest, I could just smack myself for all those unproductive busy moments. I should have been using that time to get the rest I was lacking. Come on, take a load off your back and relax. Kick your shoes off, put your feet up and relax. All that stuff will be there. Trust me, it is not going anywhere.

Take a good long look at where you are in life and begin to incorporate me time. However you decide, make a choice to give yourself some much needed attention. Find ways that will help you tune back into yourself. Do you have a hobby? Have you ever thought of one? Have you deserted a hobby you enjoyed? Remember *Me time is time I designate to myself within the day or on a specific day to retreat, replenish, rejuvenate, and rest myself.* When you are at your best you will give your best.

Now it is your turn. Today is a new day and you have been given the opportunity to start fresh. If you have identified areas of your life that you have neglected, here is your chance to make a change. Change is not always easy. As it has been said, it is hard to teach old dog's new tricks but you are not a dog. Change is inevitable if you are going to continue to grow as a woman. Change can hurt and old habits can become a challenge to break. Old attitudes are stubborn. Know that everything you desire to change you can change. Start small with the areas you have identified. The small changes will motivate you to continue to make changes in your life. God never intended for you to become complacent. Isaiah 32:9 says: *You women, who are so complacent, rise up and listen to me you daughter who feel secure, hear what I have to say.* God sent a warning to the complacent women that change was coming and for them to get ready. I believe we can become comfortable in situations that offer us just enough but not enough to be the best woman the Lord desires for us to be. We limit ourselves because we adapt too quickly to comforts and we abhor change. Invite change, invite change into every area of you life. Reinvent yourself and began to live the very best you. Remember, "You are the only you".

Self Reflections/Group Discussion

1. What does me time mean to you?

2. What changes do I need to make to experience me time?

3. Discuss being complacent.

4. What does it mean to reinvent yourself? Is it time?

5. Have I lost my creativity? How will I restore it?

About The Author

The gospel of the Lord Jesus Christ was presented to me in the spring of 1979. My heart was broken when I learned that Jesus loved me so much He died on the cross for all my sins. There at the altar I repented of my sins and received Jesus Christ as my Lord and Savior.

I am the wife of Wayne Cockrell, Pastor and founder of the Genesis Bible Fellowship Ministries in Baltimore, MD, where I have served over the years in various ministries since the founding of the church in June 1986. God blessed me to be the mother of three children, who are now adults, and the grandmother of two grandsons and one granddaughter.

I'm a woman on a mission to live the very best me through utilizing all the gifts and talents the Lord has given me and to teach, encourage, and support women of all ages to live the very best them according to the Word of God. I've had the opportunity to speak and teach over the years at various women's functions and fellowships. Nothing excites me more than to help women understand who they are and the power they have to accomplish everything God has placed in their hearts to do. So I want to encourage you to develop the character of Christ and walk in wholeness through the Word of God in spirit, soul and body and become devoted followers of Jesus Christ. This is my assignment from God.

Some of my hobbies include reading, decorating, baking, gardening, and, of course, shopping. My favorite pastime is sitting by my window with a cup of tea dreaming and my greatest accomplishments are when those dreams come true.

My life scripture has become Galatians 2:20, *I have been crucified with Christ and I no longer live, but Christ lives in me. The life I live in the body, I live by faith in the Son of God, who loved me and gave himself for me.*

"Against all odds"
Iris

My Sister,

This is just the beginning of the rest of your life. Everyday you are given the privilege and the opportunity to make choices. You have the ability to change your circumstances.

You have the power to think positive thoughts and the ability to create an environment conducive for spiritual growth. Get excited about your life. Explore every opportunity the Lord gives you. Embrace challenges with a positive attitude. Try new things. Never be afraid of change it is the catalyst used for growth and blessings. It is never too late to change. Everyday give God thanks and trust Him. Begin today living the best you. Remember, "you are the only you", take care of yourself.

Now to Him Who, by (in consequence of) the [action of His] power that is at work within us, is able to [carry out His purpose and] do superabundantly, far over and above all that we [dare] ask or think [infinitely beyond our highest prayers, desires, thoughts, hopes, or dreams] To Him be glory in the church and in Christ Jesus throughout all generations forever and ever. Amen (so be it). Ephesians 3:20

To contact the author for speaking engagements,
small group teaching or book club discussions/signings
visit the website at: www.livingthebestme.com.

Please include your testimony and how this book
helped you.